Art of the Tudors and Stuarts

Elaine Baker

Acknowledgements

The author and publisher would like to thank the Bridgeman Art Library and the National Portrait Gallery, London, for providing the pictures for reproduction.

Thanks to the following for permission to reproduce the images:

Sir Thomas More and Family:	By courtesy of the National Portrait Gallery, London.
The Ambassadors:	National Gallery, London / Bridgeman Art Library, London.
Hampton Court Gardens:	John Bethell / Bridgeman Art Library, London.
View of London:	Private Collection / Bridgeman Art Library, London.
The Armada Jewel:	By courtesy of the Board of Trustees of the V&A / Bridgeman Art Library, London.
The Ditchley Portrait of Elizabeth I:	By courtesy of the National Portrait Gallery, London.
Jacobean Embroidered Jacket:	By courtesy of the Board of Trustees of the V&A / Bridgeman Art Library, London.
A Scene on the Ice:	National Gallery, London / Bridgeman Art Library, London.
Charles I on Horseback:	National Gallery, London / Bridgeman Art Library, London.
St. Paul's Cathedral:	Bridgeman Art Library, London.
Selection of Delftware:	Bonhams, London / Bridgeman Art Library, London.
Carving at Petworth House:	National Trust, Petworth House, Sussex / Bridgeman Art Library, London.

Editor: Ian Jenkins
Illustrations by Elaine Baker
Cover by Gordon Davies of Moss Davies Dandy Turner Ltd.

First published 1994 by Folens Limited, Dunstable and Dublin.
Folens Limited, Albert House, Apex Business Centre, Boscombe Road, Dunstable, LU5 4RL, England.

Printed in Great Britain by Gallpen Press

Contents

Sir Thomas More and Family

Time Line

1478	Thomas More is born.
1483	Edward IV dies. His brother Richard, Duke of Gloucester is crowned Richard III.
1485	The Battle of Bosworth between Richard III and Henry Tudor. Richard dies and Henry becomes Henry VII – the first Tudor king.
1492	Christopher Columbus sails across the Atlantic and discovers America.
1493	Columbus returns. Pope Alexander VI divides the newly found land of America between Spain and Portugal.
1498	Vasco da Gama discovers the sea route to India.
1503	Julius II becomes Pope.
1503 – 4	Leonardo da Vinci paints the *Mona Lisa*.
1508	Michelangelo begins painting the ceiling of the Sistine Chapel.
1509	Henry VII dies and is succeeded by his son Henry VIII.
1510	The pocket watch is invented by Peter Henlein.
1516	Princess Mary is born to Queen Catherine and King Henry VIII. Thomas More writes *Utopia*.
1519	Magellan begins his world voyage.
1521	Martin Luther declares his opposition to the pope at the Diet of Worms.
1529	Thomas More becomes Lord Chancellor.
1532	Thomas More is imprisoned for his opposition to Henry VIII's religious reforms.
1535	Thomas More is executed for treason.
1565	Rowland Lockey is born.
1593	Rowland Lockey uses Holbein's drawings as a basis for his painting of Sir Thomas More and his family.
1616	Rowland Lockey dies.

Sir Thomas More and Family
by Rowland Lockey, 1565 – 1616 (after Hans Holbein).
By courtesy of the National Portrait Gallery, London.

TECHNIQUES

Rowland Lockey used drawings by Holbein as a basis for this painting of Sir Thomas More and his family. It could not have been painted from life as it was produced fifty-eight years after Sir Thomas More's death. It is painted in oil on canvas.

QUESTIONS ? ? ? ? ? ? ? ?

1. Look at the surroundings of the figures. What evidence can you find to show that this is a wealthy household?

2. This is certainly a family in which books are very important. Count the number of books you can see in the picture. Is there anything unusual about any of them?

3. There are two different styles of fashion in this picture. What are the main differences between the large group on the left and the group of four on the right?

4. Look carefully at the background of the picture. What musical instruments can you find? Look carefully at the clock. Why do you think it is painted in such detail? Look at the flowers and name as many as you can.

5. The chain that Sir Thomas More is wearing shows that he is Lord Chancellor of England. The rose pendant on the front of it symbolises the family name of the king. What was it?

ACTIVITIES

Individuals

1. This family obviously loved books. Paint a family portrait and include the family's hobbies, e.g. books, television, computers.

2. Collect some flowers and musical instruments. Draw a still-life picture like the left background section of this picture. Observe the objects carefully and paint them in light and shade.

3. Look at the clock in the painting. Design a clock for the present day – a wall clock or one that stands on a table. Discuss how different kinds of clock are suitable for different purposes, e.g. highly detailed clocks are used for decoration.

In Small Groups

4. Compare this portrait with *The Ambassadors* (picture 2) and *The Ditchley Portrait of Elizabeth I* (picture 6). List the similarities between the pictures.

5. Look carefully at the ruffs on the necks of the costumes in the Sir Thomas More portrait. Make a ruff using crepe paper.

6. Using card and foil make a chain like the one worn by Sir Thomas More. Sketch the design first, and colour it. The sketches could then be used as a border around some of the work done in the other activities.

Background

ROWLAND LOCKEY 1565 – 1616

Rowland Lockey was an English miniaturist, designer and goldsmith. He was apprenticed to Nicholas Hilliard and painted this large family portrait in about 1593 at the age of 28.

Hans Holbein had first visited England in 1526 with letters of introduction to Sir Thomas More from Erasmus. It was during this period that he painted portraits of Sir Thomas More and his family and friends. He returned to Basel for a period and came back to England in 1532, by which time most of his former patrons were either disgraced or dead.

Henry VIII, by the Act of Supremacy, had been granted by Parliament the title of Supreme Head of the Church of England. Only two important men refused to agree with Henry's demands for loyalty. One was Archbishop Fisher of Rochester, Queen Catherine's confessor and chief defender. The other was Sir Thomas More, who was the first non-ecclesiastic to hold the post of Lord Chancellor in England and a brilliant writer. In his book *Utopia* (from the Greek meaning 'no place'), More told the story of a traveller in a perfect society of peace, law, reason and beauty. As a result of refusing to obey Henry VIII, More and Fisher were beheaded in 1535.

The Ambassadors

Time Line

1497/8   Hans Holbein is born in Augsburg, southern Germany.

1509   Henry VIII succeeds to the throne and marries Catherine of Aragon.

1515   War breaks out between France and Italy.

1519   Hans Holbein becomes a member of the Basel Artists' Guild.
Charles I of Spain is elected Holy Roman Emperor Charles V.

1520   The Ottoman Empire is taken over by Suleiman the Magnificent.
Henry VIII and Francis I meet near Calais on the Field of the Cloth of Gold.

1521   Martin Luther breaks with the Papacy at the Diet of Worms.

1522   Magellan completes his circumnavigation of the globe.

1525   William Tyndale begins printing the New Testament in English.

1526   The Mogul Dynasty is founded in India.
Hans Holbein settles in England.

1529   The princes who support Luther protest the Edict of Worms at the Diet of Speyer. They become known as the 'protestants'.

1532   Henry VIII's marriage to Catherine of Aragon is declared null and void.

1533   Henry VIII marries Anne Boleyn in January. Princess Elizabeth is born in September.

1534   Henry VIII breaks with Rome and founds the Church of England.

1535   Hans Holbein paints *The Ambassadors*.
Sir Thomas More is beheaded.

1536   Anne Boleyn is beheaded. Henry VIII suppresses the monasteries in England and confiscates their wealth. Henry marries Jane Seymour. On 12th October, Prince Edward is born but unfortunately Queen Jane dies.

1543   Hans Holbein the Younger dies in England of the plague.

The Ambassadors by Hans Holbein, 1497/8 – 1543.
The National Gallery, London.

QUESTIONS? ? ? ? ? ? ? ? ?

1. Look carefully at the picture. Both of these young men are wealthy and very important. Which details show this?

2. Look at the background of the picture. The upper shelf has instruments for studying astronomy. The lower shelf has instruments for cultural pursuits. What items would you use to show the scientific and cultural pursuits of the present day?

3. Some details in this picture show the religious problems of the time. The picture was painted in 1535, after Henry VIII's break with the pope. There is a Protestant hymn book and a lute with a broken string which could indicate religious discord. Find the other musical instruments in the picture and identify them.

TECHNIQUES

Hans Holbein was a very versatile and technically accomplished artist. He painted many outstanding portraits of which *The Ambassadors* is one of his finest. This painting is in oil on wood. It was designed to hang on the wall of a large staircase. As people walked up or down the stairs the anamorphosis in the portrait would become obvious.

ACTIVITIES

Individuals

1. The upper shelf in this painting contains a sun dial. Investigate how a sun dial works and design one. It could be made appropriate to the Tudor period by incorporating the Tudor Rose and some of the heraldic patterns and symbols used by the Tudors.

2. Look carefully at the different scientific and musical instruments in this picture and draw some of them. Think about what would be their modern equivalents.

3. The artists of the sixteenth century were interested in distorting images. The strange object between the feet of the two men is a skull which has been stretched sideways. This is called anamorphosis. Create an anamorphosis using a simple picture, by drawing on a squared grid and then distorting the grid (see page 29). Remember to match the picture, square by square. The correct shape will be seen only from a particular point – in Holbein's picture, this point is at the ambassadors' eye level.

In Small Groups

4. The two men are standing on a patterned floor which is based on the Cosmati mosaic floor in Westminster Abbey. The pattern is made up of squares, circles and triangles. Draw a patterned border around a 20cm square or circle and then design a pattern in the same style as the Cosmati floor. Use only squares, circles and triangles in the design and colour it in only three colours, including black or white. A number of patterns could be displayed together.

Background

HANS HOLBEIN THE YOUNGER 1497/8 – 1543

Hans Holbein the Younger was born in the winter of 1497/8 in Augsburg. He was taught by his father, Hans Holbein the Elder. He developed a good reputation for his work and became a member of the Basel Artists' Guild in 1519. He designed print blocks for the Basel printers, painted portraits and executed church commissions.

Holbein illustrated the Lutheran Bible in 1522 and produced the famous woodcuts for the *Alphabet of Dance* and the *Dance of Death*. He moved to England in 1526, where he was employed by Henry VIII. He produced silverware and jewellery, portraits, other drawings and miniature work, and designed court costumes. He died of the plague in England in 1543.

This portrait is of two educated, powerful and wealthy young men. On the left is Jean de Dinteville (1504 – 1555). He was a young French aristocrat on a diplomatic stay in London. The globe on the bottom shelf marks his chateau at Polisy and his dagger sheath is inscribed '*aet svae/29*' (aged twenty-nine). On the right of the picture is George de Selve (1508 – 1541). He was appointed Bishop of Lavaur at eighteen. He visited his friend Dinteville in London in April 1535, when this picture was painted. His arm is resting on a book inscribed '*aet svae/25*' (aged twenty-five). He later became the French ambassador to Charles V in Venice and the Vatican.

Time Line

1520 Hampton Court is completed and is presented to Henry VIII.

1522 Magellan completes his circumnavigation of the globe.

1532 Henry VIII divorces Catherine of Aragon.

1543 Copernicus publishes *Revolutions of the Celestial Orbs.* *Structure of the Human Body* is published by Versalius.

1545 The Council of Trent undertakes the reformation of the Catholic Church.

1546 Francis I of France commissions Pierre Lescot to build the Louvre Palace.

1547 Henry VIII dies at Whitehall and is succeeded by his son, Edward VI. Henry II becomes King of France. Ivan IV adopts the title of Tsar of Russia.

1552 War breaks out between Emperor Charles V and King Henry II of France.

1553 Edward VI of England dies. Some of the English nobles, fearful of his Catholic half-sister Mary, declare Lady Jane Grey as queen. She reigns for only nine days before Mary heads an army to London. Mary is crowned queen and Lady Jane and her husband are executed.

1554 Mary I of England marries Philip II of Spain. The protestant clergyman John Foxe publishes the *Book of Martyrs*.

1555 Mary I restores Catholicism in England. Germany is divided between Lutheran and Catholic Princes at the Peace of Augsburg.

1556 The Holy Roman Emperor Charles V abdicates and retires to a monastery. The Habsburg empire is divided. Philip II ascends the throne of Spain and Ferdinand becomes the Habsburg ruler.

1558 Mary I dies on 17th November and is succeeded by her half-sister, Elizabeth I.

QUESTIONS ? ? ? ? ? ? ? ? ?

1. Look at the chimneys in the picture (this is just a small section of the roof). What does the number of chimneys tell you about the kind of building this is?

2. The garden is divided by low hedges and gravel paths to make attractive shapes. Where do you think the best view of this garden would be?

3. The low hedge is made from a bush called box which can be clipped to a neat shape. There is also lavender planted here. The lavender flowers would have been dried and used in the house to give a pleasant smell to the rooms and to clothes. Is lavender still used as scent today? What other flowers have strong scents?

4. The Great Hall in Hampton Court is famous for its hammer-beam ceiling. There are also beautiful painted ceilings by Sir James Thornhill. Name some churches or big houses that you have visited which have interesting ceilings. What are they made from?

TECHNIQUES

Set in both gardens and parkland, the palace is a superb amalgamation of fine Tudor architecture and Sir Christopher Wren's building.

Hampton Court Gardens.
Photograph: John Bethell / Bridgeman Art Library, London.

ACTIVITIES

Individuals

1. Study the design of this garden, then produce your own garden design. Base it on a central point within a square with box-edged flower beds around the centre. Think of the different colours that would be made by both the flowers and the gravel paths.

2. The Tudor emblem was a rose (see page 28). Use a piece of strong card and draw the rose carefully. Now fill in different parts of the rose with different shapes of pasta and glue them firmly into place. When the rose is finished spray it gold.

In Small Groups

3. Look at the royal coat of arms. The shield is supported by a lion and a unicorn, two of the heraldic beasts. At the entrance to Hampton Court there are ten statues of the royal beasts. Design a coat of arms and use two beasts to support it.

THE KING'S BEASTS

4. Use mod-roc supports and a base of chicken wire and newspaper to construct an heraldic beast. The design of the beast should be discussed and drawn before beginning construction.

Background

HAMPTON COURT GARDENS

Hampton Court is a magnificent palace near London. Cardinal Wolsey began building it in 1514, and it was presented to Henry VIII in 1520. It became Henry's favourite country home. His activities there included Royal Tennis, a different form of modern lawn tennis. The game is still played today on the enclosed court adjoining the palace. Henry lived there with five of his wives and the ghosts of Jane Seymour and Catherine Howard are said to haunt the palace.

The main facade of the house overlooking the gardens dates from the accession of William III in 1689, when Sir Christopher Wren was asked to improve and enlarge the building. Anne Boleyn's Gateway in the Tudor part of the house is a superb example of the brickwork of the time. It includes a wonderful astronomical clock made for Henry VIII. There are many examples of different gardens within the grounds, from the Knot Garden to the maze and the famous grape vine which was planted in 1769.

View of London

Time Line

1457	William Caxton becomes the first Briton to use a printing press.
1485	Henry Tudor becomes Henry VII, the first Tudor king.
1492	Christopher Columbus discovers America.
1509	Henry VII dies and is succeeded by Henry VIII.
1547	Henry VIII dies and is succeeded by Edward VI.
1553	Edward dies and is succeeded by Mary I.
1554	Mary I marries Philip II of Spain.
1558	Elizabeth I succeeds to the throne of England upon the death of her half sister Mary I. Elizabeth restores Protestantism.
1561	Mary Stuart becomes Queen of Scotland.
1564	William Shakespeare is born.
1569	Gerhardus Mercator publishes a world map using his famous projection.
1580	Francis Drake completes his circumnavigation of the globe.
1588	The Spanish Armada is defeated.
1603	Elizabeth I dies and is succeeded by the first of the Stuarts, James I.
1625	James I dies and is succeeded by his son, who becomes Charles I.
1642	Conflict between Charles I and Parliament increases and the Civil War begins.
1649	Charles I is defeated and beheaded.
1653	Oliver Cromwell becomes Lord Protector of the English Commonwealth.
1660	The restoration of the monarchy.
1662	Cornelius de Visscher dies.
1665	The Great Plague of London.
1666	The Great Fire of London virtually destroys the city.

QUESTIONS ? ? ? ? ? ? ? ? ?

1. The Elizabethan theatres stood beyond the city limits on the south bank of the River Thames, which was then called Bankside. Where are the Swan, the Rose and the Globe theatres in the picture?

2. Most of the buildings in this picture were made of wood and were built very close together. Why did this make things worse during the Great Fire of London?

3. The theatres on the Bankside were thought to be very bad places because some of the audiences were very poorly behaved. The theatres were closed during the plague. Why do you think this was sensible?

4. The River Thames was a very important shipping area. How many ships and boats are on the river? What were they used for?

5. Look at the number of churches in this picture. How many churches do you think were in London at this time?

TECHNIQUES

This painting is a view of London with the Swan, the Rose and the Globe theatres shown on the south bank of the River Thames. The old St. Paul's Cathedral is shown, after the removal of Inigo Jones' spire (it was twice struck by lightning soon after 1650). This dates the picture between 1650 and 1666, when the cathedral was virtually destroyed in the Great Fire of London. The remains of the structure were demolished in 1668 and Sir Christopher Wren was commissioned to design and build the present cathedral.

Beneath the picture is printed text. After 1457, when William Caxton became the first Briton to use a printing press, the printed word became more and more popular. His press worked by using moveable type. This meant that there were separate blocks for each letter which could be moved around to make words and sentences. Pictures were printed from carved wooden blocks. Before this, all books had been written out by hand.

ACTIVITIES

Individuals

1. Music was very popular in the Tudor and Stuart periods. Playing instruments, singing and dancing were all popular activities. *Greensleeves* is a folk song thought to have been written by Henry VIII and *London's Burning* is a famous song about the Great Fire. Design the front cover for a piece of sheet music for either of these songs.

In Small Groups

2. Inigo Jones was a famous architect who designed the Banqueting House in the Palace of Whitehall. Members of the king's court performed plays there called masques. The scenery and costumes were spectacular, and often the actors' identities were hidden behind masks. Masques rarely had a story but were written about the natural world and various events. Make one set of masks to represent the four seasons and another set to represent war, peace and fire.

Group or Whole Class

3. Using the masks designed in small groups, discuss and organise a masque and then perform it for the class.

4. Look at the sketch of the inside of the Swan Theatre, the largest of the Elizabethan playhouses. It was said that 3 000 spectators could squeeze into the galleries and the pit around the stage. Make a model of an Elizabethan theatre using card, wood and any other suitable materials. Some research, planning and initial sketches will be needed before starting to build the model.

View of London *by Cornelius de Visscher, 1619/29 – 1662. Private collection.*

Background

CORNELIUS DE VISSCHER
1619/29 – 1662

Cornelius de Visscher was one of many Dutch and Flemish artists who visited London during the Tudor and Stuart era. Some, like Holbein, stayed and made their homes there.

Little is known of Cornelius de Visscher's life and other work.

The Armada Jewel

Time Line

1547	Nicholas Hilliard is born. Henry VIII dies and is succeeded by his son, Edward VI.
1553	Edward VI dies and is succeeded by his Catholic half-sister, Mary.
1558	Mary I dies and is succeeded by her half-sister Elizabeth.
1561	Mary Stuart becomes Queen of Scotland.
1564	William Shakespeare is born.
1569	Gerhardus Mercator produces a world map using his famous projection.
1572	The Massacre of St. Bartholomew, when the Parisian protestants are slaughtered.
1576	The provinces of the Netherlands unite under the Pacification of Ghent and drive out the Spanish.
1577	Nicholas Hilliard visits France.
1580	Francis Drake completes his circumnavigation of the globe, during which he landed near San Francisco.
1581	The northern Netherlands declare themselves independent of Spain.
1582	The reform of the calendar is commissioned by Pope Gregory XIII.
1586	El Greco paints *The Burial of Count Orgas*.
1587	Mary, Queen of Scots is accused of conspiracy against Queen Elizabeth and is executed at Fotheringay.
1588	The Spanish Armada is defeated by a combination of the English fleet and North Sea storms.
1603	Elizabeth I dies and is succeeded by the first Stuart monarch, James I.
1619	Nicholas Hilliard dies.

QUESTIONS ? ? ? ? ? ? ? ? ? ?

1. Do you like this jewel? What do you like or dislike about it?

2. When this portrait was painted, Queen Elizabeth I was nearly sixty years old. Do you think the artist was trying to flatter her? Why would he want to do this?

3. The cover of the jewel is decorated with the Ark of the Church. The reverse of the cover has a Latin inscription and a red enamelled rose with twining green stems and leaves. Why would a rose have been used for Elizabeth I, the last Tudor monarch?

4. How do you think this jewel would have been worn? As a brooch or pendant or in some other way? It was given to a man – would he have worn it? Look at some paintings of the time to help you.

5. The inscription on the back is in Latin SAEVAS TRANQUILLA PER UNDAS (peaceful throughout stormy waves). What do you think this means?

The Armada Jewel *by Nicholas Hilliard, 1547 – 1619. By courtesy of the Board of Trustees of the Victoria and Albert Museum, London.*

ACTIVITIES

Individuals

1. Look at the shape at the top of the jewel and draw it to make a pattern. Repeat the pattern and decorate it using only three colours.

2. Roll out a tile of clay 2cm thick and approximately 12cm square. Decorate the tile with the pattern from activity 1 – either cut the pattern into the tile or build up the design on top. Glaze the tiles, then fire them and arrange them together in a group.

3. Create a design using the Tudor rose (see page 28) and the words ELIZABETH REGINA within an oval shape that could be used as a cover for the jewel.

In Small Groups

4. Design a portrait within an oval shape 6cm high. Include as much detail as possible. Use either crayons or water colours. Make a decorative surround using braid, sequins or beads stuck on to card. Mount the portrait in the centre. Make a hinged cover for the portrait.

Background

NICHOLAS HILLIARD 1547 – 1619

Nicholas Hilliard, the son of an Exeter goldsmith, held a warrant as a goldsmith from Queen Elizabeth I. Hilliard is the first native born English artist whose life and work are reliably documented. He is best known for his miniature portraits, which are invaluable historical records. He visited France in 1577 and as a result his style is very close to the French court art. Among his finest portraits are *Alice Hilliard* and *Young Man among Roses*. The latter painting shows in visual terms the symbolism of the love-story of Sir Philip Sidney, a friend of Nicholas Hilliard. Isaac Oliver was a pupil of the Hilliards', who also wrote a treatise on miniature painting entitled *The Art of Limning*.

TECHNIQUES

The Armada Jewel is thought to have been made by Nicholas Hilliard around 1588 as a gift from Queen Elizabeth I to Sir Thomas Heneage. It is now in the care of the Victoria and Albert Museum in London. It is made from enamelled gold and set with diamonds and Burmese rubies. It encloses a miniature painting of Queen Elizabeth I on vellum stuck to card. The front of the case shows a gold profile bust of Queen Elizabeth I on a blue enamelled background, and the back of the case has the 'Ark of the English Church tossed on a stormy sea', in gold and enamel. The jewel is just seven centimetres long.

The Ditchley Portrait

Time Line

1558 Elizabeth I succeeds to the throne on the death of her Catholic half-sister Mary.

1559 John Knox leads religious reforms in Scotland.

1561 Marcus Gheeraerts the Younger is born.

1568 Marcus Gheeraerts the Younger settles in England with his father.

1580 Francis Drake completes his circumnavigation of the globe.

1588 The Spanish Armada attempts to invade England.

1589 The Bourbon dynasty in France is founded by Henry IV, thus ending the religious wars.

1595 The East Indies are explored by the Dutch.

1596 The first six books of Edmund Spenser's *The Faerie Queene* are published.

1597 Western missionaries are expelled from Japan.
Hugh O'Neill leads the Irish Rebellion.

1598 Legal recognition is given to the Huguenots in France by the Edict of Nantes.

1599 William Shakespeare becomes a partner in the new Globe Theatre in London.

1600 The charter is granted to the English East India Company.

1601 Elizabeth I addresses her final Parliament.

1602 The charter is granted to the Dutch East India Company.

1603 On 24th March Elizabeth I, the last of the Tudor monarchs, dies at Richmond Palace. She is succeeded by James VI of Scotland who is crowned James I of England, the first Stuart monarch.

1625 James I dies and is succeeded by his son Charles.

1635 Marcus Gheeraerts the Younger dies.

The Ditchley Portrait of Elizabeth I
*by Marcus Gheeraerts, 1561 – 1635.
By courtesy of the National Portrait Gallery, London.*

QUESTIONS ? ? ? ? ? ? ? ? ?

1. Compare the map of southern England in this picture with a modern map of the same area. Are the towns and villages the same? What modern towns and cities did not exist in the Tudor period? Look carefully at the coastline and rivers. Are they still the same today? Why are different areas of the map differently coloured? Why does the portrait show the queen standing on a map of the country?

2. Look carefully at all the fine details in the picture. What do you think were the queen's favourite jewels? Do you think that this would have been a light dress to wear?

3. Why do you think the queen is shown carrying a fan and gloves?

4. How has the artist shown the different textures of lace, pearls, jewels, fabric and sky?

ACTIVITIES

Individuals

1. Use the patterns made by the jewellery on the dress to construct a repeating pattern.

2. There are several small ships in the portrait. This is because England had defeated the Spanish Armada only four years before this portrait was painted, and the English and Spanish navies had fought great sea battles between July and October 1588. Find out about these battles and write a short account of a day in the life of a sailor. Illustrate your account with images from the portrait.

In Small Groups

3. The ships have been included in this portrait because they were of great interest to Elizabeth I. Paint or draw a full-length portrait of a friend, including details of his or her interests and hobbies.

4. Design an elaborate costume that Elizabeth I might have worn for an important occasion. Use the repeating pattern from activity 1 as a basis for the design. Sketch the design first, then produce it using collage – fabric for the dress itself, foil and coloured paper for the jewels, thread for the embroidery.

Background

MARCUS GHEERAERTS THE YOUNGER 1561 – 1635

Marcus Gheeraerts the Younger was a well known Flemish portrait painter who had settled in England with his father in 1568 and produced costume portraits of the late Elizabethan and Jacobean periods.

This portrait was commissioned by Sir Henry Lee. He was the Queen's Champion, which meant that he organised the annual jousting matches at court in which he defended her honour. In 1590 he retired from this post and went to live at Ditchley near Oxford. Queen Elizabeth was most offended, and in an attempt to regain her favour he entertained her at Ditchley in September 1592. He commissioned this painting (which became known as 'the Ditchley portrait') to commemorate her visit and to celebrate her forgiveness.

Elizabeth I looks impressive in her jewels and ruff, despite the fact that the portrait was painted when she was almost sixty. She had resorted to wearing an auburn wig to hide her thinning hair and concealed the ravages of time on her face by a liberal use of cosmetics.

TECHNIQUES

This portrait is painted in oil on canvas and shows Queen Elizabeth I standing on a map of England, particularly of Oxfordshire, with her back turned to the storms of anger and clouds parting to show sunshine. The Latin inscriptions say that 'she gives and expects nothing in return; she can, but does not take revenge'.

Jacobean Embroidered Jacket

Time Line

1603 Elizabeth I dies and is succeeded by the first of the Stuart monarchs, James I.

1605 The Gunpowder Plot to blow up Parliament is a failure. One of the main conspirators, Guy Fawkes, is arrested.

1605 *Don Quixote* is published by Cervantes in Spain.

1606 The northern New Hebrides Islands are discovered by Quieros. The coast of Australia is sighted by Janszoon. Torres sails around New Guinea.

1607 *Orfeo*, the first opera by Claudio Monteverdi, is produced.
The English settle in Jamestown (named after the king).

1608 A French colony is founded in Quebec.

1609 Galileo builds a telescope.
Astronomica Nova is published by Johannes Kepler.

1610 Hudson Bay is explored by Henry Hudson.
Henry IV of France is assassinated. He is succeeded by his son Louis XIII.

1611 *The Tempest* by William Shakespeare is performed.
The King James Bible is printed.

1615 Manhattan Island is settled by the Dutch as a fur-trading post.

1618 The Catholic Habsburgs and Protestant German princes start the Thirty Years War.

1620 The English Pilgrims sail on the *Mayflower* and land in America at Plymouth Bay.

1624 Philip IV of Spain makes Velasquez court painter.

1625 James I dies and his son succeeds to the throne as Charles I.

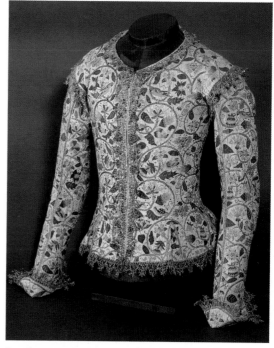

Jacobean embroidered jacket.
By courtesy of the Board of Trustees of the Victoria and Albert Museum, London.

QUESTIONS? ? ? ? ? ? ? ? ?

1. Do you like the pattern of embroidery on this jacket? Give reasons for your answer. Do you think it would have been warm or cool to wear? Why?

2. Look at some Tudor and Stuart portraits. What fabrics were the clothes made from? What does this tell you about the wealth of the people in the portraits?

3. The people in portraits of this period employed artists to flatter them and show them off to their advantage. Discuss with a partner how these people wished to be judged in the future from their portraits.

4. The ruffs worn in this period had to be starched to make them stand. Do you think they would have been comfortable?

5. How do you think clothes like this were cleaned? Were they ever cleaned? There was no piped water then. Most of the nobility carried pomanders and had pot-pourri in their homes. Why do you think they did this?

ACTIVITIES

Individuals

1. In Stuart times, craftsmen organised themselves into guilds. These are guild badges:

 Cooper's Mark    Woolmerchant's Mark   Silversmith's Mark

Each guild had a coat of arms which showed the tools of its trade. Draw a twentieth century coat of arms for a computer programmer, an astronaut or a pop singer.

2. Design a maker's mark to identify things that you make. It could incorporate your initials. Sketch a simple design and then cut it from either a lino block or a potato to use in printing.

3. Look very carefully at the patterns on this jacket and draw or paint some of them.

In Small Groups

4. Make a collage using this embroidery pattern as a starting point (see page 30). Use threads, cords or string for the stems and tissue or fabric for the flowers. Add a lace edging using paper doilies sprayed gold or silver.

TECHNIQUES

The Jacobean period was famous for its fine embroidery, sometimes using stumpwork, but often using fine sewing such as in this jacket. Many of the stitches used are still in use today, e.g. satin stitch, long and short chain stitch. The fabric would probably have been cut out and the various garment pieces then embroidered by hand before the final jacket was made up. Handmade lace would have given it the finishing touch.

Background

JACOBEAN EMBROIDERED JACKET

This is a richly decorated jacket covered in colourful silk embroidery. The neck, shoulders, front, hem and cuffs are edged with lace. The design is beautifully symmetrical with hook fastenings on the front. The colours are still clear and fresh. This jacket is typical of the extremely high standard of embroidered garments that were worn in the sixteenth and seventeenth centuries by the English nobility.

Time Line

1580 Francis Drake returns to England after completing his circumnavigation of the globe.

1585 Hendrik Avercamp is born in Amsterdam.

1589 The Bourbon dynasty is founded by Henry IV of France.

1603 Elizabeth I dies and is succeeded by James VI of Scotland, who becomes James I of England.

1618 The Thirty Years War begins.

1625 King James I dies and his son succeeds to the throne of England as Charles I. Christian IV of Denmark enters the Thirty Years War on the Protestant side. An army is created for the Emperor Ferdinand by Wallenstein.

1626 Christian IV is defeated at the Battle of Lutter by the army of the Catholic League.

1628 The Petition of Right is adopted by Parliament, asking Charles I to suspend his use of the royal prerogative.

1629 Bernini is appointed to be the official architect in charge of St. Peter's in Rome.
The Edict of Restitution is issued by Emperor Ferdinand, returning all lands seized from the Catholic Church since 1555.

1630 King Gustavus Adolphus of Sweden enters the Thirty Years War to help the German Protestants.

1632 *Dialogue on the Two Chief Systems of the World* is published by Galileo. Charles I of England appoints Anthony van Dyck as court painter.

1634 Hendrik Avercamp dies.

QUESTIONS ? ? ? ? ? ? ? ? ?

1. Look at the skates that are being worn and compare them with modern ice skates. Which type of skates do you think would be easier to wear?

2. Many different parts of Dutch society are represented in this picture, from wealthy people meeting friends and enjoying themselves, to other people who are carrying on with their everyday activities. Find the two horses which are pulling sleds. Compare the trappings of the two animals. Look at how people are carrying goods on their shoulders, suspended from poles. How are things transported differently today?

3. Look at the clothes that the people are wearing. Do they look warm? Is every person wearing a hat of some kind?

4. Find some people who have fallen over. Find some footprints. Apart from horses, what other animals or birds are in this picture? Find at least seven children – what are they doing?

Background

HENDRIK AVERCAMP 1585 – 1634

Hendrik Avercamp was born in Amsterdam and he trained as an artist there with Pieter Isaacsz. He later lived at Kampen in the province of Overijssel. Avercamp specialized in winter scenes and his figures have life and charm. Perhaps knowing that he was a deaf-mute gives the figures an explosive eloquence as they tumble, slide and go about their daily lives in this scene on the ice. His compositions are usually framed by bare trees and pinkish buildings – this is a typical example. Ice scenes in this style were extremely popular. They were composed in the studio from acutely observed water colour drawings.

ACTIVITIES

Individuals

1. Draw and paint a modern version of this picture using lots of small figures. Use the same type of composition that Avercamp used, with buildings and bare trees framing the scene.

2. Paint a winter scene with very pale shades and bare-branched trees. Look carefully at the shapes of trees and how the branches and twigs grow. Trees in winter are often quite dark and could be painted in silhouette against the snow.

In Small Groups

3. Find out about the patterns made by snowflakes and ice crystals. Design some shapes from these patterns and cut them out of white paper, then mount them on a light blue or silver background.

Group or Whole Class

4. Create a model of a winter scene. Make small figures and buildings using paper and card, and make trees using sticks and twigs. Discuss and plan carefully the location of the scene, the time of day, the number of people, what each person is doing, and the animals to be included.

TECHNIQUES

Avercamp worked in oil paint, usually on wood. He created lively and charming scenes using sensitive colour schemes. There is always a feeling of intense cold on the frozen water which contrasts well with the pinkish glow of the buildings which are usually presented at the sides and in the backgrounds of his work. The composition is balanced in a conventional manner so that even with the enormous amount of detail shown, the picture produces a coherent whole.

A Scene on the Ice *by Hendrik Avercamp, 1585 – 1634.*
The National Gallery, London.

Time Line

1599	Anthony van Dyck is born in Antwerp.
1603	Elizabeth I dies and is succeeded by James VI of Scotland, who becomes James I of England – the first Stuart monarch.
1605	The Gunpowder Plot to blow up the English Parliament is a failure, and Guy Fawkes is arrested.
1610	Galileo invents the telescope. An alliance is formed between Spain and the Holy League.
1613	Michael Romanov becomes Tsar of Russia, beginning a dynasty which ruled the country until 1917.
1618	The Thirty Years War begins.
1621	Anthony van Dyck visits London for the first time.
1625	James I dies and is succeeded by his son, Charles I.
1632	Anthony van Dyck is appointed court painter to Charles I and is given a knighthood.
1637	Charles I tries to impose the Anglican Church on Scotland. Rene Descartes' *Discourse on Method* is published, setting out his universe based on reason.
1638	*Discourses on Two New Sciences* is published by Galileo. Louis XIV is born in France.
1639	Jean Racine, the classical French dramatist, is born at La Ferte-Milon.
1640	The Great Elector, Frederick William, begins his forty-eight year rule in Brandenburg-Prussia.
1641	Anthony van Dyck dies at the age of 42.

Charles I on Horseback *by Sir Anthony van Dyck, 1599–1641 The National Gallery, London.*

QUESTIONS ? ? ? ? ? ? ? ??

1. Where is the sign which identifies the person in this painting?

2. Do you think this portrait makes the man seated on the horse look like a dignified king? How tall do you think that this man would be when he was standing up?

3. Do you think the king's armour looks heavy? Do you think the portrait is more effective because the king is wearing armour?

4. Look at earlier pictures of people wearing armour. Find differences between the king's armour in this painting and the older armour.

5. Do you think that the background of this picture is effective? The king is on a hill looking out into the distance, with the light areas behind him. Compare this portrait with the Ditchley portrait of Elizabeth I (picture 6). Which picture do you prefer and why?

TECHNIQUES

Van Dyck set a new standard for portraiture in England with his flattering and refined style. He gave almost all his sitters a look of intelligence and distinction. Charles I was not a tall man but van Dyck gives him regal dignity and makes him the perfect image of monarchy.

ACTIVITIES

Individuals

1. Design a cover for a book entitled *Ride Into Danger*. The design should include a horse and rider.

2. There is a famous triple portrait of Charles I by van Dyck which shows his head from three different angles: a three-quarter face, a full face and a side view. Draw or paint a portrait of a friend in this way.

In Small Groups

3. Portraits can be sculpted or modelled as well as painted. Make a clay portrait bust. Use either a friend as a model or base the head on that of Charles in the painting.

Group or Whole Class

4. Make a collage of an equestrian portrait. Think about the different textures needed for the armour, trees, horse, hair, feathers, and other details. Introduce as many different textures as possible.

Background

ANTHONY VAN DYCK 1599 – 1641

Anthony van Dyck was born in Antwerp in 1599. His first independent works, produced when he was seventeen, show great precocity. He first visited London in 1621, when he painted a portrait of George Gage; an agent who acquired works of art for the royal collection of Charles I.

Van Dyck left England for Italy where he stayed until 1627. He spent time in Rome, Genoa and Venice where he painted portraits and executed commissions for churches. He painted for a while in Antwerp before he returned to England and finally settled there in 1632 as court painter to Charles I, who gave him a knighthood. Van Dyck was profoundly influenced by Rubens and the work of Titian.

Charles I of England was one of the greatest royal art collectors. He relied on agents and advisors to find works for him and over a period of twenty years he amassed a collection of over 1 500 works, many of them of outstanding quality. His greatest acquisition was the purchase of the Gonzago collection in Mantua between 1625 and 1627. This included works by Mantegna, Leonardo da Vinci, Titian, Raphael, Caravaggio and Correggio.

St. Paul's Cathedral

Time Line

604 The first cathedral of St. Paul is constructed. It is made of wood and is soon destroyed by fire.

1087 The Normans rebuild the cathedral. It is the largest church in England and the third largest in Europe, with the tallest spire and steeple ever built.

1561 The Norman cathedral is damaged by fire but is later restored.

1628 Inigo Jones designs a classical facade for the cathedral.

1632 Christopher Wren is born.

1660 The restoration of the monarchy in England: Charles II becomes King.

1665 More than 60 000 people die in the Great Plague of London.

1666 The Great Fire of London destroys 13 200 homes and eighty-nine churches (two thirds of the city). St. Paul's Cathedral is almost completely destroyed.

1667 Louis XIV of France and Charles I of England became secret allies under the Treaty of Dover.

1668 Sir Christopher Wren is given permission to demolish the damaged St. Paul's Cathedral and construct a new cathedral on the site.

1672 Louis XIV of France and Charles II of England join together in a war on the Dutch.

1675 Construction of the new St. Paul's Cathedral begins.

1685 Charles II of England dies on 6th February, after being received into the Catholic faith.

1710 The new St. Paul's Cathedral is completed.

St. Paul's Cathedral, London.
Front exterior.
Photograph: Bridgeman Art Library, London.

22

ACTIVITIES

Individuals

1. The building is planned using geometric spaces. Using circles, squares and ellipses, design a pattern within a cruciform shape. Colour or paint the patterns in blue or gold.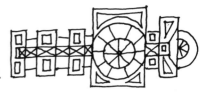

2. A famous dean of St. Paul's Cathedral was John Donne (1573–1631), who wrote the words 'No man is an island entire of itself; every man is a piece of the continent, a part of the main. Any man's death diminishes me, because I am involved in mankind. And therefore never send to know for whom the bell tolls; it tolls for thee.' Draw an outline of either the old St. Paul's Cathedral (picture 4) or Wren's design. Print these words or write them in your best handwriting inside your outline and illustrate a border around it using design features from the picture.

In Small Groups

3. The central paved area is decorated with a coloured marble compass design surrounded by a black and white design. Using a central compass, design a floor pattern in black, white and gold to fit in a circle.

TECHNIQUES

The construction of the present St. Paul's Cathedral began in 1675, according to Sir Christopher Wren's designs. It took thirty-five years to complete and cost £721 552. The cathedral is built from stone from royal quarries on the Isle of Portland in Dorset which both weathers and carves well. The overall length of the cathedral is 157 metres, its breadth is 70 metres, the height to the top of the cross surmounting the dome is 111 metres. The weight of the dome and superstructure is about 65 000 tonnes.

The cathedral's architectural style is Baroque. This combines classical lines with a strong sense of dynamic movement. This was a popular style between 1600 and 1750 and a rather controversial choice for a cathedral in London. The west front of the cathedral has two storeys of classical columns flanked by twin towers. The pediment over the columns features a bas-relief sculpture of the Conversion of St. Paul and above the pediment is a statue of St. Paul, and on either side are figures of St. Peter and St. James; these are all the work of Francis Bird (1667 – 1731). The twin towers house the bells and the clock, which has the popular name of Big Tom.

Background

ST. PAUL'S CATHEDRAL

Christopher Wren was born in 1632 and became a mathematician and an astronomer before he began designing buildings. He was one of the founder members of the Royal Society in 1660 along with Isaac Newton, Robert Boyle and Robert Hooke. After the Great Fire in 1666 Wren submitted designs for a new London. His most famous design was for St. Paul's Cathedral, the first large British church to have a dome. Of the churches in London built after the fire, fifty-two were designed by Christopher Wren. The reign of Charles II was an era of elegance after the drab and grim seriousness of Cromwell, marked by a new flourish in literature and scientific discoveries.

A Selection of Delftware

Time Line

1666	The Great Fire of London.
1685	Charles II of England dies on 6th February, after being received into the Catholic faith. His brother succeeds to the throne as James II. Louis XIV revokes the Edict of Nantes, which granted religious freedom to the French Huguenots. George Frederick Handel is born in Halle. Johann Sebastian Bach is born in Eisenach.
1687	*Principia Mathematica* is published by Isaac Newton.
1688	The Glorious Revolution occurs when James II is forced to flee to France and his son-in-law William of Orange and daughter Mary take the English throne.
1689	William and Mary are crowned King William III and Queen Mary II of England. Peter the Great takes full power as the Tsar of Russia.
1694	Voltaire is born in Paris. Queen Mary II dies of smallpox.
1700	Leibnitz becomes the first president of the Berlin Society of Sciences.
1702	William III dies on 8th March and is succeeded by his sister-in-law, Anne, the last of the Stuart monarchs.

QUESTIONS ? ? ? ? ? ? ? ? ? ?

1. Look carefully at the edges of the plate. It is possible to see the red clay underneath where the white glaze has chipped. Do you think this spoils the appearance of the plate or makes it look more genuine?

2. Plates like this often had pictures of the king and queen to celebrate the restoration of the monarchy in 1660 or the beginning of the reign of William and Mary in 1688. What objects are made now to celebrate royal occasions?

3. Do you like the cat jug? Why? What would you expect it to be used for?

4. Do some research to find out what a posset pot could have been used for.

Background

A SELECTION OF DELFTWARE

This type of pottery is named after Delft in Holland where it was first made. When William and Mary became king and queen of England, they brought Delftware with them from Holland to decorate Hampton Court. These pieces were made in England, in workshops set up to cater for the demand for fashionable pieces.

TECHNIQUES

Delftware is a tin-glazed pottery, a process which involved coating earthenware with an opaque white glaze containing tin. The techniques were brought from Italy by emigrant craftsmen in the sixteenth century. They helped to establish native traditions of tin-glazed pottery in France, the Low Countries, England and elsewhere. Dutch Delftware and English tin-glazed ware was mostly decorated in blue in the Chinese style. By the end of the sixteenth century it was in common use for drug and ointment pots, dishes, bowls and mugs.

Tulip vases were very popular items in the seventeenth century, like the one sketched here. They were used to display all types of cut flowers. It was possible to buy different sizes of vase, some of the largest being over 100 centimetres high. The flowers, birds and leaves pictured in blue on the posset pot are still in common use on Delft pottery today.

ACTIVITIES

Individuals

1. Delftware was usually produced in shades of blue and white. Using these colours design a picture of plants, flowers and birds in the centre of a paper plate. Include a design around the rim. Draw or paint directly on to the plate, or use a separate piece of paper and then paste it on to the plate.

2. Some pieces of Delftware were designed to commemorate a royal event such as a coronation, a wedding or a birth. Design a ceramic object in the style of the Delftware to commemorate a royal event.

3. Using the cat jug as a starting point, draw the cat and use it to decorate a teapot, a sugar basin, a cup and a saucer to complete the set.

In Small Groups

4. Blue and white is a popular combination of colours, particularly for fabrics and ceramics in kitchens. Design a pattern to be printed on textiles in blue on white.

5. Make a simple coil pot, and by adding feet, ears and a tail turn it into an animal jug. Glaze and fire it. If using new clay, harden the jug and then paint or gloss it.

A Selection of Delftware.
English Delft posset pot and cover, either Bristol or London, c.1700;
Liverpool Delft circular dish; English Delft jug in the shape of a sitting
cat, Southwark, c.1670. Bonhams, London.

Time Line

1648	Grinling Gibbons is born in Holland.
1660	The monarchy is restored in England and Charles Stuart becomes Charles II.
1666	The Great Fire of London.
1667	Grinling Gibbons settles in England.
1685	Charles II is converted to Catholicism. He dies and is succeeded by his brother, who becomes James II.
1688	James II is deposed during the Glorious Revolution. He is succeeded by William III and Mary II, who rule jointly.
1701	The Act of Settlement assures Protestant succession to the English throne. The War of the Spanish Succession is waged against Louis XIV of France.
1702	William III dies and Queen Anne's reign begins.
1704	The Duke of Marlborough defeats the French at the Battle of Blenheim.
1707	The formation of the union between Scotland and England.
1709	Richard Steele begins the publication of *The Tatler*.
1711	*The Spectator,* written by Richard Steele and Joseph Addison, starts publication.
1713	French dominance in Europe is ended by the Treaty of Utrecht.
1714	*The Rape of the Lock* by Alexander Pope ridicules fashionable society. Queen Anne, the last of the Stuart monarchs, dies. By the Act of Settlement she is succeeded by George I.
1720	Grinling Gibbons dies.

Carving at Petworth House, Sussex
by Grinling Gibbons, 1648 – 1720.
The National Trust.

QUESTIONS ? ? ? ? ? ? ? ? ?

1. Find the musical instruments in the carving, including the violin and bow, and the instrument that looks like a recorder. Find the musical instrument with a person's head. What other instruments are shown?

2. Look carefully at the fine detail of the carving. Find part of the carving that is of a piece of lace. What are depicted on the pendants? How would these pendants have been hung? Where are the open book and the quill pen?

3. Do you think that it would be difficult to create a carving as detailed as this? Give reasons for your answer.

4. Look at the borders down the sides of this picture. What are shown on these borders? This is one of the carvings from a large country house – Petworth House in Sussex. Find other pictures of different types of carving in different materials, e.g. stone, wood, marble.

ACTIVITIES

Individuals

1. Design a musical instrument and then make a picture of it using pieces of card in different shades of one colour. Decorate the instrument using shapes of leaves and flowers cut from card. Glue the finished picture on to a plain background.

2. Sketch some drawings of individual plants, leaves and flowers. Use pencil or pen and ink to draw the natural items as accurately as possible.

3. Stretch a piece of cartridge paper by wetting it thoroughly and attaching it to a flat board using a gummed paper strip. As the paper dries it shrinks to give a smooth surface on which to paint. Paint a musical instrument in water colours, use a background wash in a different colour, and add details with a small brush. When the finished painting is dry cut it from the board and mount it.

4. Use a spoon handle or an old table knife to carve a block of soap. Carve a small group of leaves, a cameo pendant or a face.

In Small Groups

5. Make a collage of this carving (see the design on page 31). Pad the larger instruments to give them shape. Pay careful attention to the texture, weight and colour of the fabrics used.

TECHNIQUES

Grinling Gibbons' carving has great delicacy and finesse. He preferred to carve fruit, flowers and lace motifs. There is a fine lace cravat carved from limewood in the collection at the Victoria and Albert Museum, London. When this was carved it would have been virtually white, and would have looked even more like the starched lace and linen cravat it was meant to represent. This particular carving was once the property of Horace Walpole and the story is told that he once wore it plus gloves to greet a visiting party of Frenchmen, who departed convinced that this was how an English gentleman always dressed.

Background

GRINLING GIBBONS 1648 – 1720

Grinling Gibbons was an English wood carver. He worked under Sir Christopher Wren and enjoyed the royal patronage of both Charles II and George I. Examples of his work are at Windsor, St. Paul's Cathedral and many country houses, particularly Petworth House in Sussex, where there is a magnificent room containing his carvings. Grinling Gibbons has long been acknowledged as England's most celebrated wood carver.

Art of the Tudors and Stuarts – Use a photocopy or a tracing of this page.

Anamorphosis means stretching a picture so that it looks squashed or curved.

When you look at the squashed picture, it looks strange. When you look at the picture from a certain angle, or at a reflection of the picture in a cylinder, it looks normal.

This is called anamorphic art.

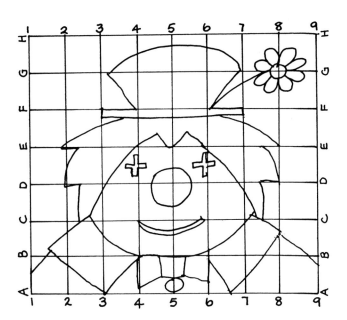

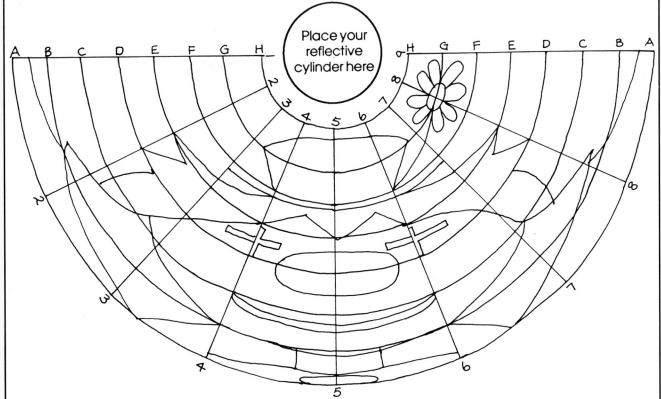

Place your reflective cylinder here

What you will need:
- for the picture: pencil, paper, ruler, eraser, coloured pencils or paints
- for the cylinder: a sheet of mirror paper (or shiny wrapping paper), scissors, sticky tape, a cylinder (e.g. a cardboard tube).

Practise stretching a picture on this grid.

Try a picture of your own using a simple butterfly instead of a clown.

Art of the Tudors and Stuarts – Use a photocopy or a tracing of this page.

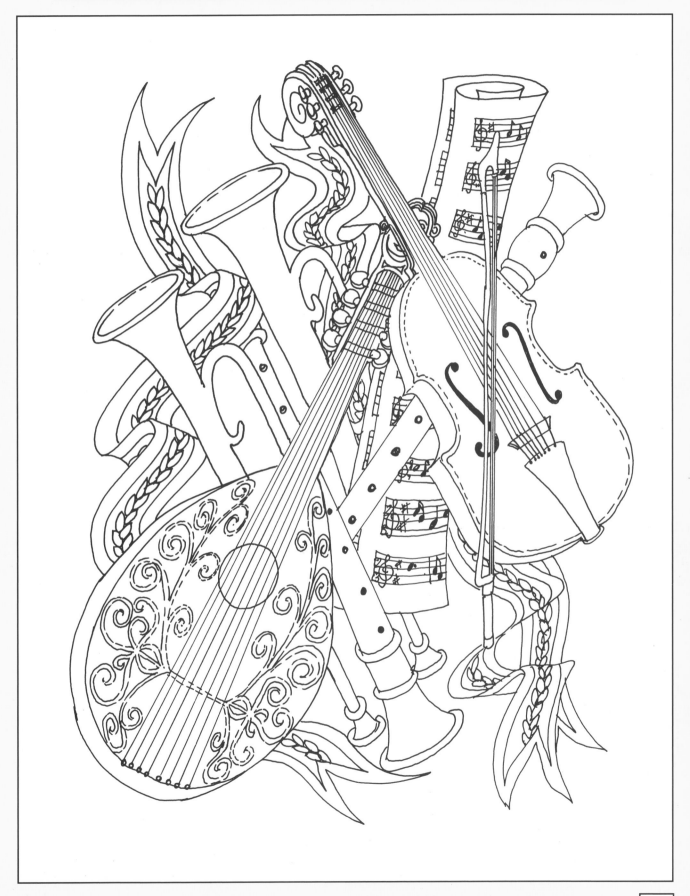

Glossary

Anamorphosis   This is taken from the Greek and refers to the distorted image of a subject shown in painting or drawing. The image can be seen in its correct proportions only from a certain point or as a reflection in a curved mirror.

Astronomy   The science of the stars and heavenly bodies.

Baroque   Originally a jeweller's term for a misshapen pearl, now a term used in art and architecture to describe an ornate and exuberant style which was in fashion from 1600 to 1750.

Bas-relief   A carved sculpture projecting only slightly from its background.

Collage   A picture made from pieces of paper and/or textiles with other materials sometimes pasted on.

Crypt   An underground chapel or cell.

Epitaph   An inscription on a tombstone.

Equestrian   To do with horsemanship, or (noun) a person who rides on horseback.

Guild   An association giving mutual support and help to its members, often comprising of craftsmen.

Hammer beam roof   A timber roof in which the rafters are supported by a series of brackets, each one resting on the one below.

Miniatures   The art of painting, usually portraits, on a very small scale. Often painted in gouache on card or vellum. By the eighteenth century miniatures were often painted in watercolour on ivory and some were done in oils on metal.

Pomander   A ball of sweet-smelling substances.

Pot-pourri   A scented mixture of spices and dried petals.

Silhouette   A profile portrait in black on white, cut out, painted or drawn from shadow.

Stumpwork   A type of embroidery using raised or embossed figures, padded with cotton wool or hair to give a three-dimensional effect.

Terracotta   This literally means 'baked earth', a hard baked clay used for statues or as decoration in architecture.

Vellum   A type of fine parchment.

Woodcuts   A relief-printing technique where the design is drawn on a flat area of wood. The part to be left white is cut away, leaving the remainder to print black.